C000261459

Poetry before anything

Newcastle Stanza Group Anthology
2020

Edited by
Roger Bloor

Clayhanger Press

Newcastle under Lyme

First Printing, 2020

Published by Clayhanger Press

ISBN-978-1-9162001-3-5

ACKNOWLEDGEMENTS

This anthology was a communal effort and I thank all the poets for contributing and taking part in the proof reading and commenting. The Newcastle Stanza Group based in Newcastle under Lyme was formed in 2018 and this anthology celebrates the second anniversary of the group.
The collection of poems demonstrates the wide range of poetic devices and forms that we workshop in our meetings.

Roger Bloor

The Poem 'Neck End' was previously published in 'Bringing It Home" United Press 2014.

Roger Bloor's poems were written during a residency at Trentham, Gardens.

Cover photographs by Alex Harford

'I will never cease advising my friends and enemies to read poetry before anything'

Arnold Bennett

Contents

Poems by John Williams

Rave Tent

Arriving early for the gigs I sit and watch
an act before the show goes on: the Tech Team
clamping amps on gantries in the roof,
three, four floods to max the woes and dreams.
Cables hum and feedback whines and whispers
from the wings like someone held in chains.
Above the flash of instant day, the moon blinks
working on the mind before it thinks.

The dead lights flicker from a finger check.
Someone turns applause to boom
and pulls the next group to the stage.
They fix a creaky song before it fails
and save the day with lightning in a click.

Stub

I keep the stub to prod my jelly pens
when the ink runs dry. Too short to grip
in sentences or spell, it writes short words,
keeps keyboards free of fluff and pulls dead staples out.
I lick the lead for luck and chew the end
and twist the stub around to taste the wood;
lips, tongue and teeth where thought is made
and letters start in lines and loops.
Wavy shavings show the sea's been up
to take the stub to carbon and the sand.

Bronze Age Cup

Ramped up in the tabloids: "Stash From the Past",
drug trace found in a Bronze Age cup.
A gift from Beaker folk to the Space Age
glows lilac in lab light that shouts heroin.
You'd think a Magus zonked in the turf house
kissed the rim and uttered an oracle.
The trace of dope that prophesied gone dry.

Much like our online psychic blogs,
the voice that needs the phone's green charging light,
touch of wood or brush with Lady Luck.
That we're still superstitious is a miracle
down to wars and woes that get to print.
We know the spectra line where heroin burns
for all the teacup dregs that talk to us.

Washing the football

The match shows up in grass stains, streaks of mud
and stud scores on the ball: the inspired play,
collapsed defence and grudge games that shed blood
remain all week until it's washing day.
The big sink, scrubbing brush and dribbling tap
bring out the scars and scuffs by must-have boots:
the nutmeg pass that laid the keeper flat,
the penalty decider in the shoot-
out in the box, grudge shrunken to a mark.
A toe-poke in the goalmouth leaves a smear,
a one-touch finish, striker's ghostly arc
still toasted in the clubhouse after years.
Most marks wash off or hide beneath the hide;
miracles show up once the game has died.

Clean Air Act

My route to low carbon led to
tomato pips in the duct-work,
dim stairs and Earth Day.
I swapped labour-slashing gadgets for hard ones,
selling the Hoover for a brush and dust pan.
A blip or a touch of sun,
I held a table sale of appliances:
incandescent lamps, pods and phones,
the bread machine that gives out gas.
Once the TV crashed, I put the screens to sleep.
Dusters shrank my footprint
and I junked the electric fan.
Haunted by the smoke genie
I learnt where the ice caps melt
and Fat Shame cards they give away in town.

Poems by Oliver Leech

Three Horses

The shortest day of the year, cold, blustery.
Past a windmill with no sails,
down tractor-track paths in a mud-lined,
    hedge-hemmed lane.
Over a gate we spied the Wrekin
slumped like a drunk on the horizon
and under bare trees, hidden by bracken and brambles,
the caves, hermit hovels, if you believe such tales.
Then, above the wide slope of a field,
sharp against the clouds, three horses,
solid and still,
as if beamed from far away
or statues conjured out of vapour,
marble out of mist.
We stared at them, they at us.
The wind, louder, gave the clouds an extra shove
and over the stile we left them,
winter apparitions,
to stay or melt back into sky.

Lych Gate

A lych gate is a roofed gateway to a churchyard to where, before the days of undertakers, friends or family of the dead carried the body to await burial and might take the opportunity there to talk about the life of the deceased.

It was one September day.
Walking near Standon, we stopped for rest
and stared across the land to hills beyond.
Then, looking down, we saw not grass
but lines of silken webbing stretched across the field,
a low-slung criss-crossed canopy,
a gossamer veil over a green bed.
Those in the know will tell, no doubt,
of money spider woven threads.
But, for a moment, imagine:
that leaves from nearby trees in their descent
find here a brief, soft resting place
where May till Autumn gamut of green,
breeze led waltzes, tarantellas in the wind
and late fanfares of colour,
all are fondly brought to mind,
a lych gate of remembrance,
before they sink and merge with soil.

Toadstool Temptation

At the edge of Bishop's Wood,
clustered in moist shade,
head heavy on stick torsos,
a phalanx of toadstools.
Plump and passive aggressive they sang:
'Pick me. Risk me.
Try me. Fry me.
Fly with me. Die with me.'
An alpha male in a single swoop
would scoop, snatch, swallow.
But I'm a lifelong danger dodger
made of timid stuff.
With just one backward glance
I walked on through the wood.
But were they poison
or once-in-a-lifetime portals
to places far, far beyond my geography?
Now I'll never know,
a thought to nag, to haunt me.

Watershed

Landlocked in Staffordshire
I walk the watershed:
    on one side Fairoak,
source of the Sow
that flows into Trent, to Humber
out east into far North Sea
merging with shallows over Dogger Bank:
    on the other Maer,
source of the Tern
that pours into Severn, to Bristol Channel
to swell the deep Atlantic
bearing eels to blue Sargasso seas.
Two raindrops, twins, on an English cloud
slip, fall, gather pace through yielding air,
side by side, close companions in descent
until, divided by a leaf,
they turn to East, to West:
one lies in haddock gills beside the Zuider Zee,
one cools toes dipped from a lilo in Guadeloupe.

Shuttlingsloe

For mountain lovers like the Swiss
to glimpse the Matterhorn is bliss;
the Japanese must feel delight
to have Mount Fuji in their sight;
Ben Nevis caught against the sky
is sure to please a Scottish eye.

You seek an English mountain top
to catch the breath and heartbeat stop?
Then past the plains of Cheshire go
and gaze in awe at Shutlingsloe,
the peak that rises stark and bluff
above the fields of Wildboarclough.

Poems by Victoria Sherratt

At Blarney Castle

And if I had kissed that stone
would all the words
in my head tumble out?
Flow as easily as a stream,
a cascade, bright splashes
over mossy stones, catch
sunlight, gain speed, volume, depth,
spread wide to become a river,
tug weed in the direction of its course,
sweep along twigs, branches,
invite other tributaries to merge
and join the river song, until
slower now but stately at their salty
entrance the sea these tumbled words
spread around the world.

Others kissed. I watched,
surprised at the ensuing silence.

Watching the Tour de France

The spiky embrace of metallic heat grasps at our bodies
under the noon sun. We share scant shade
of small trees on a parched verge.
Strangers, united in stifled waiting.
We check our watches.
Bored, sweaty children scuffle the brittle leaves.

Without warning two thunderous motorbikes
burst into the hot stillness,
after them a gushing torrent of colour and whirring wheels,
a blurred flood of focussed power fills the road

and is gone.

Poem at the Beach

Lumpy islands wait for sunset,
triangle sails slip by.
The shimmering heavy heat
suffocates the poem
until its verses venture
into the lip and lap of the waves.
The poem is refreshed,
takes shape,
takes its place
among the pink and bronzing worshippers
marooned on their multicoloured mats.
The poem beckons.

Minsmere

Three times we returned,
left bootprints on the frosty ground,
left wisps of breath in the freezing air,
iced fingers curled around binoculars.
We searched while the pale sky watched.
They're still not here. We'd better go.
The words were sitting on my tongue
when Look, look, three of them, no four.
Two pairs. Tiny egg shaped bodies
the colour of lightly baked biscuits,
black moustaches, long narrow tails,
they caused the reeds to dip and sway.
They held us on that wintery morning.
We knew nothing else.

Nothing much

says the birdman, binoculars
hung flat against his chest.
Just a single swallow.
Must've come from northern Russia.

But I hear a blackbird's question
fill the sky, fade out the hum
of traffic.

The uneven ground
beneath my boots,
the damp crushed grass,
the puddled mud.

I stop, inhale the hilltop air
watch the cloud roll back
one distant inch

to allow a spoke of sun
to pass, light up the scene.

I pull off my woolly hat,
receive the blessing
of the morning breeze.

Poems by Lyn Leech

Something Time

(Or 'be careful what you wish for')

Something always needs doing:
There isn't time
In a lifetime
For something else
To be done
Unless
You make time.
Some
Things
Are timeless
And
I want some
Time to do them
Sometime or other
Instead of all the things that have to be done
Now.

Play Lets

Bus snip chats -
'Then he said,
and you'll never ...'
Believe it I had to get off
my stop stopped the plot.

All the world's a playlet.

Mobile phones
a let-down
in the quiet zones:
Shunted trains of thought
Business-speak rattled,
Or destination never reached
From the platform of
'oh....yes.....did he.....mm...no.....
            oh.....yes.....did she......mm......no.....'
Schedule, passengers and baggage
Have alighted and left the story empty.

At Hobgoblin Gate

Shadows stretch.
Dusk crouches in the dead nettles
breathing breathing breathing breathing
in wood sorrel's ears,
thickens on tree roots.

Oaks embrace themselves -
twisted-weight branches overreach,
   fall,
      fragment
         fracture
            crumble underfoot:
fungus-filled, ankle-turning strew.

At Hobgoblin Gate
bushes brush and gather -
reel in - all paths to darkness.
Coarse grass whispers of
the lost, betrayed to
Night's silent deeps,
no moon, no stars.

A twig snaps

Speed read:

Middle page syndrome.
Scan jam
Paragraphsentences in word-
Gobbling brain gulps.
Sink, and swim in Dickens, Austen, folk tales, Kureishi,
'Pearls before Poppies'-
Prose browsing
Caterpillar omnivore.

Don't wake me
With a jolt
From the spell.
The fix.
I might drown in real life.

The shock of the view

Antidote to Country File Calendar

Mould, mildew-moist, infests all corners
and nostrils.
Blackbird corpse, (screaming, spring kestrel-taken behind my
back)
bone-frosted under skeletal shrubs.
I saw the maggots writhe there in the summer,
Constant behind my eyes, proto flies.

Flies, black, crisply juicy squashed -
Harrying the ears, the eyes.
Midges, wasps, horseflies -
Tiny tormentors,
     innumerable they fizz and buzz and swarm and rise.

Stale fox poo clumps the shoe
glutinous in decayed leaf flesh.
Forget cute mice in apples,
What about rats?
Nature's disease-ridden rats,
  Urine-soaked rodents,
    under a shed, 'near you.'

Blue-green algae,
toxic not scenic,
wriggles with larvae.
    And as for leeches -
Don't go there.

For the back-drop:
Grey damp drizzles.
Mud swamps the view

Japanese Raku

Grasp the smooth swirl of biscuit-clay
- bowl: turned, open-mouthed in amazement,
palm-nested, a made thing.
Its creaminess invites.

Glazes.
Blue, green, white - Milky silica flux
of metal oxides.
An apothecary's brew.

Stir, fill, swill, pour.
Dip.
Fingerprints left like treetops along the line
   As eternal as the pot
   As ephemeral as clay.

Hell burns it to white ice, incandescent.
Redeemed by Devil's tongs,
vengeful, it flames embracing wood.
Acrid.

Transmuted cream to black, green to bronze -
Its final incarnation
  Unforeseen.
Its existence
Baptised with tea.

If broken
Its imperfections

Were healed with gold

Poems by Julia Franklin

'C' FEVER

I must down a 'C' again - a cappuccino- and a pie,
And all I ask is a tall cup and a stick to stir it by,
And the real kick of coffee strong and my white hands shaking,
And a choc mist on the 'C's' top and the muffins baking.

I must down a 'C' again, for the call of the caffeine tide
Is a wild call and a clear call that may not be denied;
And all I ask is a plastic lid to save my drink from flying,
And a serviette and a cardboard sleeve to keep my hands from
frying.

I must down a 'C' again in this Costa Starbuck life,
With a panini and a big baguette I can eat with a plastic knife,
And all I ask are coffee shops from Inverness to Dover,
And a quiet sleep on a leather couch when the big 'C's' over.

LOADED

Serene, Queen Elizabeth from a distant sofa,
Sits and calls for honey for the Palace teatime,
And for corgis called Ivory,
Jackanapes and Prufrock,
At Sandringham there's seed cake and gin laced with lime.

Costly Spanish Footballer steaming down the pitch now,
Dribbling through the oppo and their palm-green shorts,
With an earful of diamonds, a Man-bun with amethysts,
And aftershave called Love Island, he bursts through and scores.

Choking British Highways with unfilled, unwise cracks,
Littered with detritus of a million takeaways,
Where our cars go on diesel,
Road rage, angst-led,
Fired with frustration and a deep malaise.

CHIMENEA BOADICEA

Chimenea Sturdly-Meakin lifts a mighty hand
And the doors slide back like soldiers, their queen's to
command
And the shoppers down at Tesco stand back in shock and awe,
All gloss and wheels and whirring noise, she rides to the shop
floor.

Chimenea's Danzig JXL's "A Prince of grace and power",
Its awesome speed a breathless 25 kayems an hour,
With an automatic gearbox and automatic brakes,
It conveys Chimenea to the fresh-baked bread and cakes.

Chimenea parks her trusty steed, diagonal in the aisle,
Her tattoos warning others that they'd best not cramp her style,
She hops off, fleet and nimble, (her seat rotates and slides,)
And sauntering off to make her choice, she flicks her hair and
glides.

She climbs aboard, reverses and zooms off to Health and Body,
Showing off her drinks holder, she gargles coke and voddy,
Scooping up shampoos and creams, she crams her scooter's
spaces,
She flicks her lights to High Beam and drives fast to far-off
places.

At last she's done her shopping, Danzig's loaded to its height,
She steers her way to payment, queues all melt away in fright
She drives straight past the checkout girl, she waves and glares
her smiles,
'Oh, I never carry money. I'm the Queen of all the Aisles'.

Poems by Sheila Tams

Believe in Yourself

It's no use thinking of if only
Here and now has to be the way
The past is in the past now
Just live your life each day

Let your mind wander if you want
But don't take things as read
You'll learn to let your thoughts go
And not to keep them in your head

Enjoy the simple things in life
Get out and go for a walk
It helps so much to give a smile
And to listen as well as talk

The sunshine makes you feel good
Take deep breaths and enjoy fresh air
Singing birds and fragrant flowers
Let the wind blow through your hair

Don't despair in how you feel
Don't do everything to the letter
Be confident and believe in yourself
Trust that things will soon get better

Life and time are precious
You really have come far
The futures what you want it to be
Just believe in who you are

It's Stormy Outside

Looking out of the window
At the branches on the trees
A well-orchestrated movement
Conducted by the breeze

The sky is dark and gloomy
Not the slightest bit of blue
Rain dancing on the pavements
Car wipers conducting too

Feeling warm and cosy indoors
And watching some TV
It may be stormy outside
But it's fine in here for me

Neck End

Being a lass from Lancashire
I never thought I'd find
I'd end up living in Staffordshire
Having left the past behind.

So here I am in Longton
Known as 'Neck End' my husband says
He was born and bred here
And remembers the good old days.

There were coal mines and many pot banks
It was a very thriving town
I couldn't believe there were 200 pubs
Most of which have been knocked down.

It reminds me of asking for directions
How the old folk used to say
Turn left or right at this pub
You would always find your way.

Last but not least is local dialect
Sadly another fading trend
I couldn't understand 'May un Mar Lady'
But I got there in the end.

So keep hold of our Town Hall
What's left of potteries, kilns and pubs
Let's be proud of Longton duck
And what 'Neck End' means to us!

Remembering Trentham Gardens

When I was a schoolgirl in Altrincham
And aged about 9 or 10
I came by coach to Trentham Gardens
How posh did I feel then?

I stood on a bridge by the entrance
Reading a sign for the "River Trent"
I watched the babbling water flow
And wondered where it went?

I remember a trip on the steam train
Speeding past bushes around the lake
Train seats folded back again
For the return journey you could make.

Journey's end was the swimming pool
How exciting the chute if you dare!
When you got back to the station
You could enjoy all the fun of the fair

A beautiful grand hall and gardens
Led to pergolas with roses so sweet
Afternoon tea with scones and jam
The little pots were such a treat!

You can still visit Trentham Gardens
Now known as "Trentham Estates"
It's a lot different than I remember
But it really is still great!

The Diet Starts Tomorrow

Have you seen Will Power?
I'm afraid I have to say
I really need to find him
As I think I've lost my way

My taste buds crave for chocolate
My thirst buds need red wine
I really must stop eating cake
Though I must say I feel fine

I'm bordering overweight now
I need to exercise some more
If you should see Will Power
Please send him to my door

Poems by Mike Fisher

Atlantic Challenge

'Skipper! on deck!' 'The kite's blown!'
Shredded - red, black, green and white,
Torn remnants through the letterbox,
Then stowed below,
Straight-way hoist the number three.
Within minutes, calm, the winds divide
Sails flap, 'hold steady or we gybe'

Thai curry in a yellow bowl,
Atlantic Ocean take-away
Passed hand to hand along the cockpit,
Comes with spoon.
Replete, the empty bowls passed back.
Below, the galley sink, on gimbles, forty-five degrees
Tests washers, wipers expertise

Horta beckons, three days out
The rain comes down as
Water drips from off the helmsman's nose.
Unexpected, music fills the boat and deck
And lifts the mood, maintains morale
As thoughts of Peter's Bar and solid land
Intersect with concentration on the task to hand

Shropshire Spring

Gold dust spreads across the seat
And will not brush away
Pollen falls from hazel catkins
Out the hedge row cut this day

Home from sister's Shropshire farm
The tall, tailed twigs, attest
To air that's fresh, a day that's free
Spent muddy, mindful and unstressed

High on cluttered mantel shelf
The vase has sat some days
When leaves appear, a spring-time green
Though half expected, still amaze.

The Quarry

Form IV, we learnt of millstone grit
And sandstone heaved from out the sea.
Today pebbles smoothed by passing feet, tumble the unwary.

Birch and stunted oaks enfold the slopes
And yellow flowers of gorse,
Proclaim a time for kissing, always here.

In heather undergrowth, a pheasant hides
Above a buzzard circles' and below
The sparrows hop from twig to rock to shrub

A laceration in the hillside, memories
When my son climbed up the quarry side
Ignoring risk, adventure uppermost.

Today, he fears for me,
The virus crown shapes social isolation.
More distance than these forty years.

Inhumanity to madness

1800
Straps and Iron padlocks,
Hold and bind the lunatic
Brutalizing all

1968
A secure padded cell
Schizophrenia grins across at me
Shut in together

2020
Drugs are now supreme
Bind constrain and hold the patient
Rooms and padlocks gone?

Poems by Alex Harford

Drip

drip

drip

I pull up my armchair
beside the sink and stare

How can a dripping tap leave me entranced
when I can't watch the rain?

Drip
drip
drip

I press my fingers
hard into my ears

Why does the plop of a dripping tap grate
when I love the rain's pitter-pat?

Drip
drip
drip

I lean in
sticking out my tongue

Why is the chill of a dripping tap dull
when I love a rain shower's mizzle?

Drip
drip
drip

Thunder   fractures

thoughts.

I stumble outside,
close my eyes
Pummelled
by the rainstorm.

Standing \
Off b*alance*

Stolen

Beautiful;
This is not a dreamy delusion –
it is *not* a hazy hallucination.
Sun shines from blue skies
bewitchingly blemished by white-wisps;
an unimagined paradise.

Serene;
Sprinkling, splashing, dousing, washing –
nourishing water hushing,
traversing with ease, for it is free.
A smell so cool and fresh, cup your hands
and taste purity.

Air, water, flower and stone in harmony create perfection.
The Garden of Eden's far-richer relation –
flourishes of heathers and trees and grass,
Shangri-La's European cousin, but this one is real –
a green utopia of untouched elation.

Breathless;
If I wasn't below the clouds,
I'd believe this was heaven.

Boom!
Angered skies
overcome by greys.
Rain cascades – thunderstorm!
This gentle white spout
escapes its boundaries,
crashing irrigations
flooding the plain.

The falls have stolen my heart;
My heart can stay.

Mask I

She wears it like night.
She wears it to frighten you.
She wears it airtight.

Mask XIX

The most inhumane
thing about this pandemic:
Not seeing your smile.

Mask VI

You remove the mask,
be who you deserve to Be.
Individuality.

Poems by Roger Bloor

Written during his Residency at Trentham Gardens

For Wilf

I follow close
the paths of other times
and in those narrow walks
my shadowed solitude
is lightened by the memory
of when we walked together
in this very place

John Warland's Waves

The waves –
rain rusted steel
arch and break
in seas
of prism-splintered flowers

April

Beneath an early April sun
the gardens bloom with children
buggies
dogs and rucksacks
knapsacks
picnics
walking sticks
anemones
fritillaries
and promises of summer
still to come

Miss Elizabeth

(The Miss Elizabeth boat at Trentham Gardens £2 each way)

I saw Miss Elizabeth set sail today
pulling away from the landing stage
no bands or cheering crowds to see
the boat untie and sail away
no passengers against the rail
to wave farewell to native shore

Turning with ease she left the dock
then gathered speed and headed north
soon rounded the distant island head
and then at last was lost to sight
her epic voyage begun

Who knows what travels and adventures
lie ahead for those intrepid travellers
who paid two pounds to board

Trentham Gardens

The flowers turn their heads
in stunned amazement
admiring the colours and the vast
array of forms and styles of hats
that blossom in the summer sun

Wide sombreros
Soft hats – Hard hats
Baseball caps on back to front

Floppy felt and Panama
Outback – Laid-back
Fancy – Plain

Knotted hankie
Fold up – fold down
Lacy – Racy
Boater and Cloche

But then the winner of the show appears
a gold medal bloom without a doubt
the red-hot poker
bald and sunburnt
no-hat gent
in the midday sun.

The Poets

John Williams studied English at Durham, taught English in schools and colleges and lectured in English at the University of Chester. He has published three poetry collections, 'Reading Lesson in the Lifers' Wing' (Peterloo, 2009), 'The Model Shop' (Waterloo Press 2011) and 'On Lipstick Beach' Poetry Plus' (2016). He is the Stanza rep for the Staffordshire Stanza.

Oliver Leech, Oliver Leech, born and bred in Newcastle-under-Lyme, a retired teacher of English and
Philosophy at a local school, busy with calligraphy, art, writing in different genres, unadventurous cooking, gentle walking and struggling to learn clarinet and a foreign language. His book, 'Quandaries', a collection of poems, calligraphy and artwork is published this year by Clayhanger Press.

Victoria Sherratt grew up in rural Wiltshire, studied French literature and language at Manchester University, and taught for a number of years. After bringing up four children and co-leading a church she trained as a relationship therapist. Turning to poetry in later life her poems mainly reflect her personal life as a woman, wife, mother, grandmother as well as topical issues. She also admits to a sideline in comic verse!

Lyn Leech - now over 70, spent part of her childhood travelling abroad with her parents. After she graduated from Manchester University she taught English in Sussex and then returned to Staffordshire to teach, marry, lecture and raise three children. Now retired, Lyn enjoys poetry, art, fiction writing and freehand machine embroidery.

Julia Franklin - After a few years working in radio and TV, Julia is now an actor specialising in voice work. For the last few decades, she has been recording audiobooks for some of the UK's largest publishers and although she hasn't counted them all, she estimates about 750 titles so far. Books and writing have been a lifelong passion, so she feels very lucky to be earning her living this way. Julia did an MA in Creative Writing at Manchester Metropolitan University and the novel she produced, appeared as Turn Up for the Book in 2012. With other students on the course she recorded their novels and hers - they're all on Kindle and Audible, published by her (very small) company, Books Are Loud. The second novel is coming along......slowly. In the meantime, she is writing poetry too.

Sheila Tams – Has always liked poetry and began writing around the age of 10. Inspired by Rupert Bear books and later by Pam Ayres. Sheila enjoys writing 'witty ditties' for birthdays, leaving do's and special occasions.

Sheila recently retired and is pleased her interest in poetry has been rekindled. Having her poem "Neck End" included in 'Bringing It Home' published by United Press in 2014 was a great achievement. Meeting the poet in residence Roger Bloor at Trentham Gardens inspired Sheila further and led to her joining the Newcastle Stanza Group.

Mike Fisher - Born in 1944 in Birmingham. George Dixon Grammar School Birmingham Medical School at University Birmingham then moved to Stoke on Trent for house jobs. Manchester for a psychiatry job but wisely joined a General Practice in Newcastle under Lyme.

Alex Harford - As well as writing (poetry and short stories in all sorts of genres), Alex Harford enjoys lots of things, including visiting places that don't seem real, the outdoors, photography, reading, films, 90s video games, tickling shoebills under their beaks and lots of music. Alex is also a member of Congleton Writers Forum. His poetry and flash fiction have been published in various local anthologies, and he has a website at https://AlexHarford.uk

Roger Bloor returned to his native North Staffordshire in 1984 and has published his poetry in a variety of magazines and anthologies. He is the owner and sole employee of Clayhanger Press and joint founder of the poetry magazine 'The Alchemy Spoon'. He won the Poetry London Clore Prize 2019.

.

Clayhanger Press

www.clayhangerpress.co.uk

64

Printed in Poland
by Amazon Fulfillment
Poland Sp. z o.o., Wrocław

61501742R00040